good grief

brianna pastor

brianna pastor

contents

i chose not to name these poems or put them
in any particular order. if i name them, they
stay with me. i put these poems out into the
world as a releasing -- a releasing of old
patterns, traumas, and habits that i no longer
wish to carry with me. while these poems
will always be special to me, they were
written during some of my lowest points. i
will keep them there and go back to honor
them when necessary. essentially, this book
is a symbol of growth. thank you for
walking beside me.

trigger warning:

the contents in this book discuss topics such as mental health, depression, and trauma. 'good grief' is a collection of poems and short essays that were written over the last ten years--in my journey through some of the darkest times, and the most hopeful times. read along with me, as i write to navigate my walk through self-worth, identity, depression, loss and growth. i want this book to hold you warmly, as a reminder that you are never alone, and that you are loved. i wrote this for me, but also very much for you.

the skin on my body healed itself in four days. that is how i knew that we are meant to overcome devastation, and that we complicate it by hanging onto what is no longer hurting us. we cling to pain like a parasite to its host.

with the proper care, i have avoided any infection. i was not going to allow further suffering for a small wound that burned so terribly in the moment.

we don't know how long our pain will last. we assume that because it hurts now, it is probably going to hurt tomorrow. it may even hurt the next day. perhaps it will get worse. but we sleep, and you see, and we do this marvelous thing in our sleep--we mend. and tomorrow is not always what we thought it would be.

a friend once described me as 'flammable'.
as soon as i heard the word from her mouth,
something inside of me blew apart.

it could mean many things.
but this is when i realized that it's just as
easy
to set my soul on fire
as it is to watch me come crumbling down.

i return to ashes either way.

the sun was my most-dreaded morning
routine.
one aspect i could not change,
no matter how many attempts at
opaque curtains
i had draped over-top of each other.
it was hard to tell whether music made me
feel sick
or if it reminded me of how happy i could
have been
if only i had sung along
the way my sadness sang with the birds--
persistent, with purpose, and sharp.
there are distance runners that start in my
chest,
down my arms and legs and for
every mile they run
a coach tells them to make another round.
how do i get up and start the day
when there are people who run for miles
and i just run away

i am growing backwards
a dark spiral into the opposite direction and
so different from all the others
there are no branches for you to hang onto
just a simple me, an emotion tree
not growing for you to
grow off of or to destroy
leave me be, so i may grow
strong,
on my own
and i will be my own damn home

letting go is actually the easiest decision we can make. we become so adapted to the weight of our heavy hearts that becoming *light* again is a foreign concept.

i knew that i needed you to be present.
a subtle hug in my times of agony
to feel like every act of love you gave me
wasn't for someone else's entertainment

(i am not your burden)

my therapist insists that every situation or
emotion that exists in my life
revolves around you

who am i, if you cannot love me?
are my feet worthy of the ground i walk on?
do i deserve to take this walk, even if it is
alone?

avoidance is the only way you knew how to
love me
and this was once the only basis in which
i knew how to love myself

i know you squeeze into
tight spaces with the hope that
you may fit without aching
there are spaces meant for you
that will not require you to
bend in order to belong safely

brianna pastor

it is safe to say that
nothing is safe
besides this moment
and yesterday.
that is why
we touch it

do not look me in the face.
my apologies, if my weak cheekbones
offend you today-
i haven't quite been myself.
perhaps my bones have begun to
take the form of the pillow i have made my
home.
or became concave from the incessant
inhalation of cigarette,
after cigarette,
after cigarette.
there is no beauty here.
no romance in my toxic solace.
i do not find comfort in the
excuses i spoon-feed to you,
i cannot cover up my lethargy
in grandiose, theatrical performances
to spare you the
i don't know how to help her
or the
oh no not this again

brianna pastor

i loved my sadness
because
it was honest

you need both the light and the dark. one does not exist without the other. to sweep your darkness under the rug is to do yourself a great disservice. there is so much there to learn. how can you feel the freedom of the sun when you have not sat for a while under the shade of the trees? surely, you can learn to appreciate both. it is learning to accept and exist in each state. to appreciate and welcome each part of you without discrediting it. we are creatures of light and dark. that is where strength and softness make a blood pact.

your split ends
and my split ends
are not the same.
my split ends suffer
immeasurable breakage
even after i trim them off,
and always at the most
desperate hours
of the night

i am alive to learn and unlearn, to relearn and unlearn and learn again. i am here to unpack and develop and understand the value in struggle. i am here to hold my grief the way it deserves to be held, for as long as that takes. i am here to learn that there is no judgment where there is love. i am here to understand that i am not small. i am here, and i am learning that this is a big thing.

i tend to resonate most
with people who forget that they are
loved
it's almost as if we forget that
we are living an experience
we get so caught up in the world around us
that we forget there is a worthy one
within us
i feel the need to remind each of you
that you are loved
even if you feel lost between both of them

my boundaries are not up for discussion or
debate
they are a clear, sturdy fence and
all of the sudden
you have the energy to jump them

i grow tired of your yearning excuses
that coincidently, you love on me
when i don't need it to survive
anymore

you claim to have raised me to be
the strong one
when i find myself needing to be that
for myself, against you,

only then are you
kissing your teeth for it

brianna pastor

i wrote delicate love notes to the Earth / on
my six-year-old, worn-out converse / in
hopes that when i walk / she may hear my /
incessant trying / an apology / to make up
for / how heavy / my steps were / i hope that
she understands / i hope that in her heart, she
forgives me

a couple of years back, i got the chance to
ask one of my abusers how it felt to know
that he had shoved my face so deeply into
the mud that i am still pulling bits of soil
from my teeth.

he told me that i should have known better
than to open my mouth.

i gave my sadness a full name
so that i stop thinking of her as an intruder
and start acknowledging
that i do have to learn how to live with her

brianna pastor

there is a constant duet in my head
a voice so soft, and one
an uproar:
both singing; reaching, for some kind of
peace
and even on my most harmonious days,
i'm not sure that it ever finds me

brianna pastor

i'm sorry
you cannot wake up
at the crack of dawn
every morning
contemplating your best scheme
to make your amends with me
i have laid awake
between four cold, uptight walls
every night for twenty-seven years
contemplating my own worth
and existence
because of you
if you ask me,
my burdens outspeak your guilt
actually,
i don't know
your burden just might be
too much for me to ever carry
had it been my own

i am not sorry for what you chose to do
or not do
with your love

this body was my very own
first place of residence
it did not need some fixing,
it needed to be appreciated
for the home it was

my body screams
*please don't mind the mess,
i swear it's not always like this*

my heart screams
*come in and
love me regardless*

brianna pastor

i remember being five years old
i remember the shadow that never left me

where am i? why am i here?

every voice i heard was strung
in hatred, in misery, in shielded fear
carved, now, onto the insides of my skin

your words.
you didn't hear yourself when you were
speaking.
a poorly written song with a catchy tune
the song that always seems to be stuck in my
head
and crawls back to me out of the blue

and when times are really fearful,
i can even dance to it

brianna pastor

i tend to unravel
thread by thread
like a ball of yarn.
stretched out, bare
and unruly
ready to be woven into blankets
to keep other people warm

'no' is also an action
let it be your own approval
of disapproval
wear it around your neck as you
lift your chin to turn away
even if your skin feels different
even if 'yes' tries to follow
up the back of your throat

i take great comfort in knowing
that there are even better versions
of myself
that i haven't hugged yet

brianna pastor

i want to love the universe the way it has not
loved me

just because you called out my name
and i did not speak
does not mean that i was absent
we are not children in a classroom
i do exist
without your acknowledgement
i am here
even if you do not see me

you broke my heart so many times
i spent so many years after you
trying to find a bond
without the defeat
only to learn that the bond
was a leash

brianna pastor

and then there was six-year-old me
dishing out cries in acronyms with sharpie
marker
across my wooden bunk bed:

IHTW
IHTW
IHTW

my mother questioned why *i hated the world*
when i hadn't even slightly touched it yet

my only explanation
is that i hated the parts i had already seen
why would i want to see more?

for a very long time i had disgusted myself
because i didn't say 'yes'
but i didn't say no.

i thought,
"is this what love feels like?"
and then learned that it wasn't.

you told me not to chew on bottle caps
because you didn't want me to ruin my teeth
but you had no problem in watching me love
people who were no good to me

there was one night i had found myself
stumbling into my regular coffee shop to
write. it was my safe space. i sat down in
front of a napkin that someone had left
behind. it read, "un jour, je découvrirai le
secret pour que mes yeux soient moins
lourds. ils ne guérissent jamais des pleurs."

i took out my phone to translate:
"one day i will unlock the secret to having
my eyes feel less heavy. they never heal
from the crying."

i sat in place and silently mourned. not only
did i find the answer to why i kept ending up
in this coffee shop alone, but i felt empathy
for a world that is sad *in so many different
languages.*

i never know what to say when people ask
me about myself. i have never been good at
letting someone know me before i have the
chance to worry about them knowing me.
maybe that is a bad thing. maybe i know that
i'm more than they could handle. maybe i
know that not many people can appreciate
somebody whose peace comes with a
somber aftertaste. maybe i don't know the
simple way to tell them that i'm the person
who dreams during the day and gets one or
two layers thinner at night. sometimes three.
have you ever met a person who walks
slower next to the man in the wheelchair on
the sidewalk because she feels sick to her
stomach that she might make him sad? i
haven't--i just know that i am more than
what others want to expect of me. that they
might look at my heavy face and try to read
it like hieroglyphics. and i know that they
probably wouldn't understand.

i dread the day these demons come back for
me
like they had gone away to pursue better
things
but can never find what they're looking for
so here they come, back to me,
a place where they are not wanted
for they always overstay their welcome and
don't understand the concept of *manners*
in another person's home

i am the one mistake you made
but you have never wanted to learn from me

brianna pastor

i could never be a teacher
i'm much too tired of being the one people
learn from
i've never been a fan of repeating myself
how come no one ever listens the first time

there will be no more
spreading myself thin
across my bedroom floor
to have everything
covered at once
i have split myself down
into enough layers
to cover this floor like tile
for nine of my lifetimes

brianna pastor

i swear the entire sky was on fire when you
died
i thought to myself:
this is how she would leave the world
i can't think of a better way for her to be
here
and there
and everywhere else
she can see the entire world from above
before she leaves it
better than it had ever left her

i'll be damned.
you really were too good for
what you were given

brianna pastor

there is nowhere to run to
and so much to run from
i study so much about the process of trust
but i am literal enough to know
you cannot trust a single, tangible thing
not with anything important, anyway
and everything big and small
is best kept between my two ears
and swarming around my chest
and twitching in my legs
and buzzing at my fingertips
and crying in italicized letters

i put my Grief in the corner
between the dusty nightstand and
a pile of clean laundry
Grief concentrates on the line that separates
each wall
and how many accidental scratches she can
find
to pass the time
and her legs wobble after the first two hours
Grief eventually does grow tired
despite her consistency
don't turn around
don't turn around
she closes her eyes and stretches
leans her head against the corner
Grief asks if she is allowed to have dinner
but
you don't feed Grief
Grief feeds you
don't you know better than to speak?
it's time for a nap
as the hours go by, she counts the corners in
the room,
she checks them for random scratches
and asks from underneath the door
if she might be allowed to eat
she never heard back
so, i learned to sleep
i learned it was the only way for me to leave

my mind became a castle in the sky
musing together events i know could never
happen
afloat in the ocean
a body of a much bigger form than my own
that of which i am not accustomed to coping
against.
but, i manage
and i lay there, with no worry in the world
of whom i may be
or who i may not
what i can solidly remember
and the pain i thought i forgot
the crisp severity of the ocean on the outers
of my skin
a rivalry counteracting the heat my anger is
ceaselessly producing
an effortless breath of cold air
and no endurance needed to fight against the
current
my head being totally consumed by waves,
in intervals
but enough to refresh my inner cognition.

one deep inhale and i can feel you,
just before i start to slowly fade under
and when i think this can't get any better,
i finally hear it. the thunder.
it's loud, and i've been waiting, and i am
scared

but not worried enough to budge
the storm is growing strong above my
physical, still body
and with the moving body below me that i
want to love so much.

what i can't grasp fully, though, is the way i
refuse to move
i know i am terrified of the consequences,
i'm already worrying
as i have been, this entire time

time figures out that it's not my body that
refuses to move
it is manipulated by my mind.

i am content here.
if i stay in this opposing body
it reminds me of all the things i do not have
rather than the things i do and can't accept.

i am saddened, that my breaths were not
voluntary
they were forced by the love i cannot feel.
i know it's there, i know it's real.
reminded by this ocean,
i am very much alive.

and although, inside, i may feel broken and
numb,
sometimes, i can be fine.

you can't always make a contingency plan
for when you lose yourself
because you never usually see it coming
and we are never
really prepared for it
normally, you just sink right in
and convince yourself that you'll
begin again
why do we hold on to what we were before
when did we stop looking at who we are
today
and proving that it matters more?

i'll never be as young as i am right now
at this very second
this is all there is
there is where i am
i am okay with not being okay all the time
i am okay with not having a plan

good grief, you are lazy. that's what she
always tells me. you spend so much time
asleep that you can't possibly still be tired.
that's what you think. little did she know
that in my dreams, i ran around town trying
to salvage what is left of me. i searched far
and wide for something to rescue me. to put
an end to me. be a friend to me. *good grief.*
she says i have too much time to think. i
don't know what more she expects from me.
i was made to have this body but this body
keeps rejecting me. *good grief.* she says she
doesn't know how to help me. for once i can
say that we don't disagree. i wish you could
have been my eyes when i couldn't see. this
wasn't something i could pretend to be.
depression took everything away from me.
good grief.

brianna pastor

it is said that the cells of me
once existed in the bellies of my ancestors
that i was predestined to be here
before i was ever an ounce of a thought
if these insecure legs
and rigid elbows
existed long before i hated them,
perhaps i should give them a chance
to be as beautiful as their origin

do you fear me? love asked.
no.
i fear that of which inhibits you.

1. maybe if i number what i am trying to tell you, you will take it as something you need to get done
2. you have always been good with making lists for yourself
3. i need you to know that i have never felt like my life has mattered to you
4. your form of nurture only consists of asking me mundane things at the end of the day and suggesting i call my doctor
5. almost nobody i know is ever a healthy body with a constant headache
6. i list things out for you but mostly for myself
7. the numbers remind me that there have been too many cries and not enough breakthroughs

brianna pastor

abandoned tree trunks sprawled out across
the yard
remnants from last year's party still down by
the river
i sit up from bed at five in the afternoon and
light my cigarette
i have already missed the daylight
sweet, sweet daylight, i hate you
people live during the day and become who
they are at night
i see a yellow-lit window off into the
distance
every night i watch the man in the room
dance ballet in his robe
and leave for work in the morning in a fancy
suit
i want to know who you are in the dark
*i want to know who you are when you have
nobody*

a month to this day, i turned 30. i never envisioned this happening. when i was 9, i thought i knew everything there was to know about the world. i thought that to be 30 was to see more of the same despair and i didn't think that was something to look forward to. you may know me at 30 now. but you must first know me at 9. skin and bones, fear and tears, shame for being alive. a burden to walk. a burden to feel. a burden to every life i touched. you must know me at 19, when i had nowhere to go and a new truth when i understood that i was gay. you must know me at 24, when i lived in a place where i washed my dishes in the bathtub because i couldn't afford a place with a kitchen. you must know how many times i had to put the dishes down to cry into the floorboard. you must know how quiet that was from my chest. you must know me at 30, what it has taken to get here. what has been taken from me, to get here. you must know that i awaken every day and fight through the trenches of absolute hell to keep going. it has been one month since i turned 30. and because i never envisioned this, it means that maybe i get to create it. maybe i get to create a different story to tell thirty years later. and that is something i can envision now.

brianna pastor

and if nothing else,
please,
let your love be bigger
than your anger

there is no magic answer for how i ended up
in a better place. but i can tell you how hard
i pushed to get here. i started to pay attention
to the way i greeted people, how i interacted
with them on a daily basis. i started paying
attention to the way others treated me. i
started making sure the questions i brought
to the table meant something. making sure
they weren't empty. accompanying my
smile with my eyes. having heart for others
even when mine was hurting. i read a lot of
books. and i mean, a lot of books. i wanted
to learn about myself through something
outside of myself. i read things i didn't fully
understand so that there was room for
interpretation. i became quiet and started
watching those around me. i became quiet
and i started to listen. pretending that i
couldn't hurt enough for me to not listen to
others. realizing that it was my choice to
make: loving others despite personal
circumstances. i lost a lot of people in many
different ways. i suffered deeply for those
losses. i would be lying if i said that some of
those losses weren't because i was mentally
struggling. i asked myself important
questions. what do i value. what kind of
person would i be most proud of being. what
do i enjoy. i found that community was

important to me because i never had it. i
learned to answer my questions. at the end
of the day, everything came back to the
importance of love. proving to myself that
this love also included more of it for my
own being. that, without that, my love for
others wouldn't be as whole as i intended for
it to be. i want to make the most of my
ability to love, so i began with myself. every
day. even if i didn't fully understand what
that looked like. regardless of how difficult
it was to learn.

if anyone is magically going to appear
and just suddenly make your life better,
just know that person is always going to be
you

there are people waiting to meet you.
people waiting to love you.
there are places that stand still
until you've stepped foot in them.
something really beautiful
could happen for you in the morning.
there is so much waiting for your arrival.
arrive there.

what you don't think about when you are
stuck in a pattern is how fluid your thoughts
are. we tend to grab onto thoughts as if we
are running around catching fireflies in the
dark. what we forget is that they are meant
to exist and fly and carry on. our thoughts
are just as transient. we must allow them to
flow without feeling as though we must cage
them and be caged by them.

i spend a generous amount of time
trying to convince myself
that i am worthy of taking up space
in a world
that i find myself
constantly
needing space from

my soul.
i am still learning my way to her.

i will tell you one thing, though.
she has grown like hell.

your growth will be more apparent
when it is being tested

on days where everything feels like too much, you are not abnormal. what is abnormal is denying yourself the compassion you would give so freely to others.

you know what i did? i said 'okay'. i can
feel this sadness and allow these thoughts
today, but i won't let them stop me. so i
acknowledged these thoughts and how they
made me feel—i said them aloud. myself &
i had a wonderful discussion about how i
need to be softer. so i whispered, "okay, feel
it, but we're not going to sit in it". and the
more i talk with myself, the easier it is to lift
myself out of my anguish. i kept going. i
said 'okay' to my uneasy feelings.

brianna pastor

stare hard at the hurt
ask why it stings
dig into the root and rip it out
it does not have to stay there
just because it grew there

brianna pastor

i am
hell-bent
on loving my hell

loneliness can be opportune for learning
radical acceptance of your core self. it can
be disguised as sadness when we are not at
ease with who that may be.

please do not rush my recovery
i am in a whirlpool of 'should be, could be,
would be'
when all i need
is to 'be'

to heal is to turn yourself inside out to make
amends

i know that i am terrified of loss. as if it
could end me. as if it almost has. i live on
the idea that things can stay 'okay' within
myself if we could freeze the 'okay'
moments. but the truth about moments is
that they are fleeting, so fast that perhaps
they aren't real. like this moment, right now:
it is so far past us already that i figure, well,
maybe we should just stay in this one. we
are losing moments as we speak, without
realizing that they are not tangible. even
when they deeply touch us. loss is flowing.
this moment is all we have, really. and i
want to love it, even if i lose it.

my heart will follow your heart to all ends of
the earth / like a competitive game of
musical chairs / like the flame of a candle to
oxygen / like a hopeful family to a missing
child / i will never give up on you / our souls
overlap like a Venn diagram / we have been
finding each other in circles for the last
several lifetimes / i'm not letting you get
away in this one

brianna pastor

i have gone to sleep sad so many times i'm
surprised i haven't woken up invisible yet

brianna pastor

you had your 'upper hand'
jammed so far down my throat
that i was so focused on
how i was going to breathe
and forgot that i had hands of my own
to stop you

pick it up. let it rest beside you. then, let it
be.

i know that you have loved me to the
capacity at which you know how to.

i love you for that.

brianna pastor

i remember
i think i always will

even as a child
time always stood still

i want to forget--what a concept.
are we meant to remember?

i think i'm meant to remember.

and so, we meet here, in the place
between everything light and dark
there will always be safety here for you
because i have created it for me
and for all the intricate versions of ourselves
that we will ever be

Printed in Great Britain
by Amazon

19868609R00048